## ALL ABOUT INSTRUMENTS

# PERCUSSION

### INSTRUMENTS

by
John Wood

Minneapolis, Minnesota

**Credits**
All images are courtesy of Shutterstock.com, unless otherwise specified. With thanks to Getty Images, Thinkstock Photo, and iStockphoto. Recurring – paw, Visual Unit, Trikona. Cover – Quang Vinh Tran, StockSmartStart, H.Elvin, Vec.Stock. Page 2–3 – stockphoto-graf. Page 4–5 – alexandre zveiger, De Visu. Page 6–7 – Chromakey, Hep Town, CC BY 3.0 <https://creativecommons.org/licenses/by/3.0>, via Wikimedia Commons. Page 8–9 – goldpierre, Roland Godefroy, CC BY 3.0 <https://creativecommons.org/licenses/by/3.0>, via Wikimedia Commons. Page 10–11 – the palms, Matthias G. Ziegler. Page 12–13 – Boris Medvedev, Loco Steve. Page 14–15 – ANGHI. Page 16–17 – furtseff, Zachi Evenor, CC BY-SA 4.0 <https://creativecommons.org/licenses/by-sa/4.0>, via Wikimedia Commons. Page 18–19 – sirtravelalot, SeventyFour. Page 20–21 – The Swedish History Museum, Stockholm from Sweden, CC BY 2.0 <https://creativecommons.org/licenses/by/2.0>, via Wikimedia Commons, Maria-Kitaeva, Andrew Glushchenko, Afrumgartz. Page 22–23 – De Visu, James Kirkikis, joseph s l tan matt, Igor Bulgarin.

**Bearport Publishing Company Product Development Team**
President: Jen Jenson; Director of Product Development: Spencer Brinker; Managing Editor: Allison Juda; Associate Editor: Naomi Reich; Associate Editor: Tiana Tran; Art Director: Colin O'Dea; Designer: Kim Jones; Designer: Kayla Eggert; Product Development Assistant: Owen Hamlin

*Library of Congress Cataloging-in-Publication Data*

Names: Wood, John, 1990- author.
Title: Percussion instruments / by John Wood.
Description: Fusion books. | Minneapolis : Bearport Publishing Company, 2024. | Series: All about instruments | Includes index.
Identifiers: LCCN 2024007072 (print) | LCCN 2024007073 (ebook) | ISBN 9798889169673 (library binding) | ISBN 9798892324779 (paperback) | ISBN 9798892321136 (ebook)
Subjects: LCSH: Percussion instruments--Juvenile literature.
Classification: LCC ML1030 .W66 2024 (print) | LCC ML1030 (ebook) | DDC 786.8/19--dc23/eng/20240213
LC record available at https://lccn.loc.gov/2024007072
LC ebook record available at https://lccn.loc.gov/2024007073

© 2025 BookLife Publishing
This edition is published by arrangement with BookLife Publishing.

North American adaptations © 2025 Bearport Publishing Company. All rights reserved. No part of this publication may be reproduced in whole or in part, stored in any retrieval system, or transmitted in any form or by any means, electronic, mechanical, photocopying, recording, or otherwise, without written permission from the publisher. Bearport Publishing is a division of Chrysalis Education Group.

For more information, write to Bearport Publishing, 5357 Penn Avenue South, Minneapolis, MN 55419.

# CONTENTS

Join the Band. . . . . . . . . . . . . . . . . . . . 4
Instruments from History . . . . . . . . . 6
Making Sound with Percussion . . . 8
Drum Kit . . . . . . . . . . . . . . . . . . . . . . . 10
Tabla . . . . . . . . . . . . . . . . . . . . . . . . . . 12
Cajon . . . . . . . . . . . . . . . . . . . . . . . . . . 13
Steel Pan . . . . . . . . . . . . . . . . . . . . . . 14
Mbira . . . . . . . . . . . . . . . . . . . . . . . . . 15
Timpani . . . . . . . . . . . . . . . . . . . . . . . 16
Rattles . . . . . . . . . . . . . . . . . . . . . . . . 18
Marimba . . . . . . . . . . . . . . . . . . . . . . 19
Spoons . . . . . . . . . . . . . . . . . . . . . . . . 20
Junk Percussion . . . . . . . . . . . . . . . . 21
What Will You Play? . . . . . . . . . . . 22
Glossary . . . . . . . . . . . . . . . . . . . . . . . 24
Index . . . . . . . . . . . . . . . . . . . . . . . . . . 24

# JOIN THE BAND

Do you love music? Have you ever wanted to play an instrument? Let's join a band!

This book is about percussion instruments. These instruments are often used to make a beat that the music follows. Percussion instruments are among some of the oldest on Earth.

**Musicians** in a band often play different instruments.

# Instruments from History

People played bone flutes tens of thousands of years ago.

**40,000 YEARS AGO**

**ABOUT 4,500 YEARS AGO**

Some of the oldest string instruments are lyres.

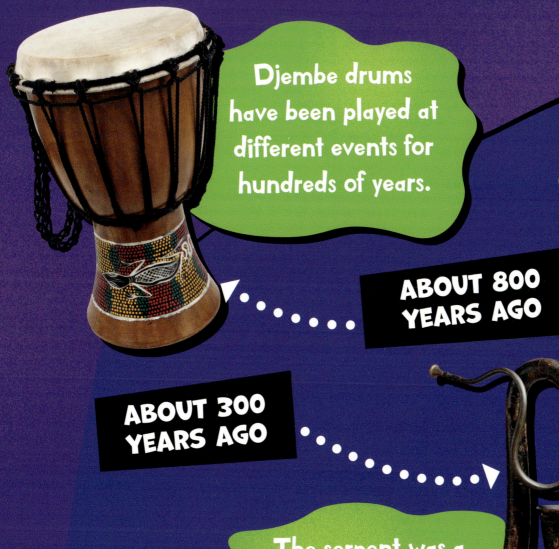

Djembe drums have been played at different events for hundreds of years.

ABOUT 800 YEARS AGO

ABOUT 300 YEARS AGO

The serpent was a popular instrument in the 1700s.

# MAKING SOUND WITH PERCUSSION

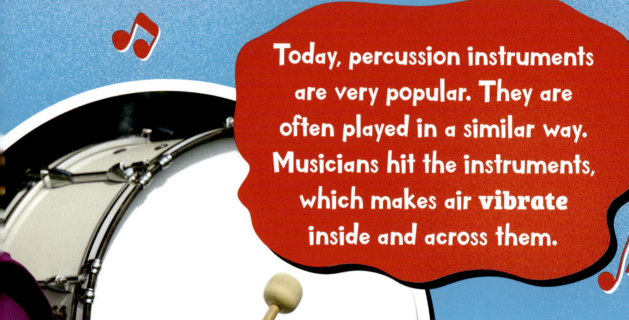

Today, percussion instruments are very popular. They are often played in a similar way. Musicians hit the instruments, which makes air **vibrate** inside and across them.

You hear the vibrations from percussion instruments as sounds.

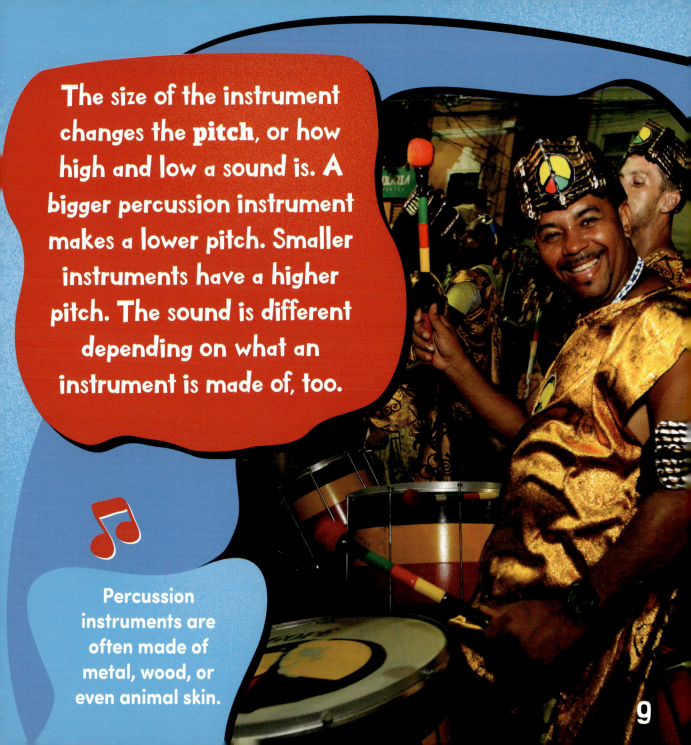

The size of the instrument changes the **pitch**, or how high and low a sound is. A bigger percussion instrument makes a lower pitch. Smaller instruments have a higher pitch. The sound is different depending on what an instrument is made of, too.

Percussion instruments are often made of metal, wood, or even animal skin.

# DRUM KIT

SNARE DRUM

BASS DRUM

CYMBAL

A drum kit has many percussion instruments in one. There are often snare drums, bass drums, and cymbals. Musicians use sticks and pedals to hit the different parts of the instrument.

**NANDI BUSHELL**

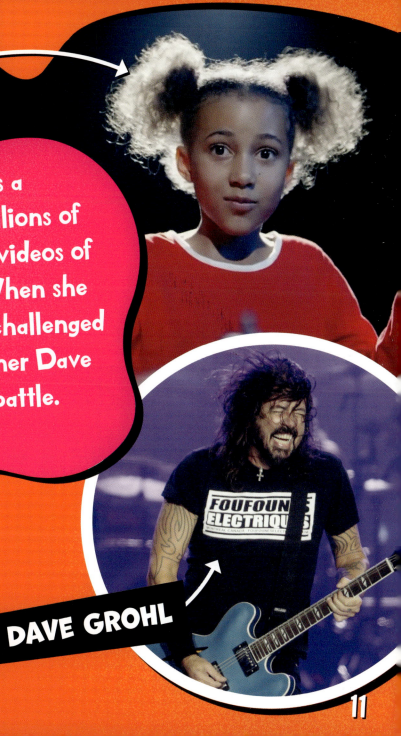

Nandi Bushell is a British drummer. Millions of people have watched videos of her playing drums. When she was 10 years old, she challenged world-famous drummer Dave Grohl to a drum battle. She won!

Nandi Bushell has played on stage with famous bands, including Dave Grohl's band, the Foo Fighters.

**DAVE GROHL**

# TABLA

The tabla is a pair of drums. The one on the left is called bayan and is often made of copper. The drum on the right is called dayan and is usually made of wood.

BAYAN

DAYAN

You play the tabla by hitting different parts of it with your hands.

# CAJON

**TAPA**

A cajon (ka-**HONE**) is a **hollow** box-shaped instrument. Players sit on it and hit the tapa, which is the front of the box. Different sounds are made by hitting different parts of the tapa.

Cajons first came from Peru but are now played all around the world.

# STEEL PAN

PLAYING SURFACE

A steel pan is a metal drum that came from Trinidad and Tobago. It has dents around the inside of its playing surface. Each dent makes a different **note** when hit with a **mallet**.

DENTS

The first steel pans were made from recycled metal objects, such as car parts or cookie tins.

# MBIRA

**METAL KEY**

**SOUND BOARD**

The mbira (em-**BEER**-uh) is a small instrument. It's played by plucking metal keys with your thumbs and index fingers. The longer keys make low-pitched sounds, and shorter keys make high-pitched sounds.

Some mbiras have beads or bottle caps that make soft buzzing sounds.

# TIMPANI

SKIN

KETTLE

FRAME

Timpani are large **kettle** drums that are usually made of copper or brass. Their tops are covered with a skin. These drums can be **tuned** to different pitches by changing how tight the skin is.

To play timpani drums, musicians hit them with mallets.

# RATTLES

Rattles are instruments that you shake to play. They are filled with small, hard pieces. The pieces make noise when they hit one another and the sides of the instrument.

Hosho are rattles made from fruits called gourds. The dried gourds' seeds shake around inside.

# MARIMBA

A marimba is made of wooden bars that are different sizes. Each bar makes a different pitch. The bigger the wooden bar, the lower the pitch.

**WOODEN BARS**

Players hit the bars with soft mallets.

**LEG**

# SPOONS

Percussion instruments can be made out of everyday things. Some musicians hold two spoons with their backs together and bounce the instrument off their hands or legs. The spoons hit each other and make sounds.

Special spoon instruments are made to be like two spoons stuck together.

# JUNK PERCUSSION

Some people use pots, pans, or junk as percussion instruments. Each thing makes a different sound.

A big empty jug can make a good drum.

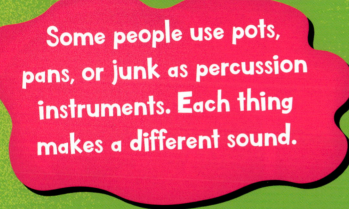

# WHAT WILL YOU PLAY?

Now you know all about percussion instruments! Pick your instrument and join a band.

Drum kits are part of many kinds of music, including heavy metal.

Brazilian music, such as samba, uses snare drums and other percussion instruments.

Highlife is a type of music from Ghana. Drums are a very important part.

Classical music uses lots of percussion instruments. Often, classical percussionists play many instruments during a concert.

It's time to start playing!

## GLOSSARY

**deaf** not able to hear

**hollow** empty inside

**kettle** a large pot

**mallet** a stick with a head that is usually large and round

**musicians** people who make or play music

**note** a musical sound of a certain pitch that lasts for a length of time

**pitch** the highness or lowness of a musical sound

**tuned** adjusted the musical pitch of something

**vibrate** to move back and forth very quickly

## INDEX

**bands** 4–5, 11, 22
**Bushell, Nandi** 11
**copper** 12, 16
**drums** 7, 10–12, 14, 16, 21–23
**Glennie, Evelyn** 17
**Grohl, Dave** 11
**hands** 12, 20
**mallet** 14, 16, 19
**pitch** 9, 15–16, 19
**skin** 9, 16
**wood** 9, 12, 19